A COFFIN IN EGYPT

BY HORTON FOOTE

★

═════════════

★

DRAMATISTS
PLAY SERVICE
INC.

D1087695

A COFFIN IN EGYPT was originally presented at Bay Street Theatre, Sag Harbor, New York, June – July 1998. It was directed by Leonard Foglia, with the following cast:

MYRTLE BLEDSOE .... Glynis Johns
JESSIE LYDELL .... Mindy H. Washington

A COFFIN IN EGYPT was first developed at the HB Playwrights Foundation, where a studio production was presented in 1980. It was directed by Herbert Berghof, with the following cast:

MYRTLE BLEDSOE .... Sandy Dennis
JESSIE LYDELL .... Bonita Griffin

CHARACTERS

MYRTLE BLEDSOE

JESSIE LYDELL

DELIA

PLACE

Egypt, Texas

TIME

1968

A COFFIN IN EGYPT

The lights are brought up on the sitting room of Myrtle Bledsoe. It is a small room with a few very handsome pieces in it: a red Chinese chest, a bookcase, a Chippendale American secretary, a small sofa, a small winged chair, a tea table in front of the wing chair. Myrtle, ninety, is still very handsome. Erect and tall, remarkably well-preserved. She is exquisitely dressed in a long red silk dress. Her skin is clear and still quite unwrinkled, and her snow-white hair is worn up on top of her head, accentuating her graceful neck, the firmness of her facial structure. She has several handsome rings: a diamond dinner ring, a ruby and diamond ring. She wears a diamond bar pin and pearls around her neck.

This is the sitting room of the house she came to as a bride. The house is surrounded by cotton fields and is part of a vast plantation. Myrtle, at rise, is seated in the wing chair looking out the window and listening to the singing, which comes from a nearby Negro church. Her companion, Jessie Lydell, sits on the sofa looking at a fashion magazine. The two women listen to the music. Jessie turns the page of her magazine.

MYRTLE. I remember that night so well. How many years ago? *(Jessie closes the magazine.)* It was a Sunday night, and across the fields I could hear the Negroes singing in their church. None of us ever went to church here in this house. Hunter had no religion one found in the churches in Glen Flora or Harrison. Can you hear the Negroes singing? I never cared for their singing, myself. I am not sentimental about Negroes and their religion as many whites I know are. I don't dislike Negroes. Some I like. Some I don't like, just as some whites I like and many, very many, I don't like. Oh, I know I am supposed to be bitter toward the Negro race, because of the colored mistress Hunter had as a young man. A young man? He preferred colored women until he was forty-five, and then he changed. "Why did you change?" I once asked him. The change almost cost him his life. But from the time he was forty-five on, he only took white mistresses. Common and vulgar, mostly, they were, too.

(Rear projection: a young, very lovely, mulatto girl.) I always thought the mulatto, Maude Jenkins, was the most beautiful, and in some ways the most refined, although when she left him for Walker, the gambler, she ran a house of prostitution, the vamp, across the tracks in Harrison. She has a house in California now, someone said. Left for there after the gambler, Walker, was killed. She's gotten fat, they say, and lost her looks. I only saw her twice when she was a girl, and she was beautiful then … Copper-colored. She looked like the Tahitian girls in Gauguin pictures. She was a Jenkins. Maude Jenkins. Her mother was the mistress of Cy Merriweather and so she was his child, they say. She was some white man's child, that's for sure. Anyway, I went to Europe because of her. *(Rear projection: Myrtle, as a young woman, with her two daughters standing beside her.)* I took my two girls and stayed eight years over there, traveling around from city to city.

(Rear projection: Algerian male in traditional Sheikh costume.) When I was in Algiers, a Sheikh fell in love with me and wanted me to divorce Hunter and marry him. He was dark-complected and my girls thought he was a colored man. He was an African, of course, and perhaps he did have colored blood somewhere down the line, as they say. Anyway, we traveled all over: Paris, Rome. My girls took ballet lessons. In New York I met Mr. Frohman and he wanted to put me on the stage. I was a close friend of Lily Cahill's sister, and Lily was sweet to me when I was in New York. *(Rear projection: Lily Cahill as a young actress.)* Lily Cahill is an actress. Was an actress. She's dead. She died of a broken heart in San Antonio, Texas, because she couldn't get a job in New York acting anymore, and she came home at the age of sixty-five to her sister in San Antonio, Texas, and tried to start an acting company of some kind, but San Antonio was in the throes of all that mess about unpatriotic books being in the public libraries. And Lily said what you had to go through in San Antonio, Texas, to put a play on was worse than ten Broadways. She died broke, they say. Proud, but broke. Her cousin was Katherine Anne Porter, the writer. Do you know her?

JESSIE. No. I've never heard of her.

MYRTLE. You never heard of her? My! She's a very good writer, they say, although I've never read her. Lily thought highly of her talent. Did you see the movie *Ship of Fools? (Jessie shakes her head to signify she hasn't.)* No? Neither did I. But you've heard of it? Well, that was based on a novel of hers. I think it was a "Book of the Month Club" selection. I can't remember anything else she's written, although I have some of her books around here some place. *(She glances over at the bookcase, then back to Jessie.)* Anyway … I was gone a long time: New York, London, Paris, Rome. And then I came home. I took my girls and came home. I've never known why. But home I came. And it's like I was never, never away. It's like that person with those two young girls, floating around Europe, around Africa, was someone I read about, or was told about, someone I knew once a long time ago. *(She looks around at the room.)* This wasn't my home, you see. *(Rear projection: Hunter as a young man.)* This is Hunter's home. He was born here. Not here in this house he built this for me — but across the road in the old plantation house was where he was born. I was born not far away though, in Eagle Lake. In the town. Not in the country. *(Rear projection: photograph of Myrtle as a young woman.)* And I was a beauty.

JESSIE. You're still beautiful. Very beautiful. A queen … a princess …

MYRTLE. Oh, thank you. Thank you. No, I'm not modest. I know I have a certain style now, a certain handsomeness, people tell me that, and I take care of myself, in spite of my age, but still, but still, it's not the same. Then I had remarkable beauty and I was much sought after by the eligible young men, and then this country bumpkin, short, strong as a bull, that's what my family kept telling me, oh, so very rich, came courting. Why? That's what I have asked him so often. "Why me? What did you see in me? My beauty? My intellect? My background?" And he stares at me and shrugs his shoulders and walks away, because he doesn't know. He found me cold, he told me once. My beauty was a cold beauty … too narcissistic, he said of me once when he wanted to hurt me …

But I was beautiful. And I refused to live on here and be humiliated while he lived openly with his mulatto woman, Maude Jenkins, who he once told me he loved better than his wife, who he wrote love letters to. Love letters that she would read aloud when she was drunk to the young white boys in Harrison that came to her house of prostitution. *(A pause. She goes to the window.)*

I'll tell you this though, when I came here as a bride, the country out here was extraordinary. I never tired of looking at its beauty. I would get on my horse early in the morning and ride for miles across the prairies; there was nothing here then for miles, no houses, no fences. The open prairie ... in the spring the wildflowers blanketed the land, bluebonnets and Indian blankets and black-eyed Susans and buttercups and primroses, miles and miles of them thick and tall and I would head east and ride through the wildflowers toward the rising sun. In the late afternoon I would ride toward the west ... toward the setting sun, and you have never seen such loveliness as there was then out here on these prairies. And sometimes when the girls were little and he would stay out all night with his mulatto mistress in Harrison ... I would go across the prairies, when the moon was full, and cry and cry; because I didn't want to cry in the house where my girls or the Negro servants could hear me.

Once, when I was young and couldn't stand the humiliation, or thought I couldn't, I went to visit a friend. I told her I could bear it if he denied it, lied to me even, but denied it; but he denied nothing. He told me he loved her. And when I asked him if he wanted me to divorce him, he said, "It doesn't matter to me. I can't marry her anyway, unless I left here, because there is a law in Texas against black and white marrying." And he wouldn't leave here. Like he said, he would put a fence around all this if he could and keep everybody but himself out. He wouldn't leave here to marry any woman, black or white, and so I left. I was gone seven years, off and on, but I told you that, didn't I?

Some friend, some long-ago, very kind friend, once told me that his father, old Leon, once remarked, "I don't know why any of them want to marry when they can have any nigger on the place for twenty-five cents." Or was it fifty cents? He thought, too, this was the world, this plantation, his father, old Leon, did ... the beginning and the end of everything. He thought all you had to do was to ride your horse through the cotton fields all day and see that the tenants and the hands worked. He thought you should learn to read and write and count money, if you were white, but only if you were white. That any other kind of education was ridiculous and a waste of time. And that all the Negroes needed to know was to farm and work and he could teach them that. And, of course, he thought it would all stay the same. Once the Yankees had gone away, even though we lost the war, he thought since they had survived, that's the father I'm talking about, he was the son of the man that settled the land first, came here from Alabama with his slaves, a hundred and twenty, I believe. Anyway, he, the father, used to say, since they had survived the war and the loss of their slaves without losing an acre of their land, they could survive anything — low cotton prices, fires, drought, floods, storms, hurricanes — and they did until the thirties and the Depression and they couldn't give their cotton and their cattle away. That's when I had to leave Europe and come home for good.

The girls were grown by then and Lois got married to a man from Atlanta. He was unfaithful; she found out during her second year of her marriage. It broke her heart, and Lorena married a boy from Houston and they went to live in the East. And I came back here, alone in this big old house with Hunter. My father-in-law was dead by then, my brother-in-law and his wife lived in the original plantation house and my other brother-in-law and his wife, the one whose son killed him, built a house over there, and my sister-in-law, Sally, built a house on the corner. And so when I came home, I was surrounded by them and their children, who were all younger than my children, but I wasn't congenial with the wives. Oh, I didn't dislike them, but we weren't congenial and they thought I was snobbish and perhaps I was. Anyway, I went to Rockport and took some lessons and I came home and began to write poetry and paint.

(Rear projection: Degas ballet dancer.) I remember once this famous dancer from New York came out to see me. She was visiting someone in Harrison at the time and they were on their way to attend a service in a Negro church out this way; we have so many I forget which one. And they stopped by to see me and to see if I wanted to go with them. But I decided not to. I asked them back after the service for tea, and when they came back I had taken every picture in the house down and replaced them all with Degas prints of dancers I had, and I must say that dancer lady from New York seemed surprised and pleased. I told her my best friend in San Antonio was a cousin of Katherine Anne Porter's and she had never read Katherine Anne Porter either, but had heard of her. She spoke French and we talked together in French. Turk, our cook, called in all the servants to listen to me outside that door there, as they had never heard French spoken before. Always after that, until the day Turk died, and faithful she was too, every once in a while she'd come up to my door and ask me to say something in French for her. I offered to teach her, and she said no. She was told it might put a spell on you if you learned something like that.

I said to her, "Turk, it's put no spell on me."

But she still wouldn't learn and I thought afterwards maybe she thinks there is a spell on me, and maybe there is. But if there is, it was there long before I learned to speak the French language, long before. Anyway, back here I was, Degas prints and all, and it was the Depression. Not that we had to do without, living out here, except we were short of money and Hunter said he couldn't afford for me to go traveling about the world, with or without my girls. And that I would have to be content out here in the country. And so I came back. I was lonely and I cried a lot, at first, but then Mrs. Carter moved out here with her children. She lived in one of the tenant houses and her husband managed the plantation store for Hunter. And they were poor as Job's turkey, but she was an educated lady from Mississippi, whose husband was shiftless and had no ambition, spent his time away from the store raising gaming chickens and taking them all over Texas for fights. Anyway, she was sweet and friendly and she wrote poetry, too. We got to visiting back and forth and she had so many troubles that it helped take my mind off of mine. I could confide in her, the way I couldn't to my sister-in-law, or to my own family, about how bitter I felt over Hunter's neglect of me.

And it was then I heard somehow that the mulatto, Maude, had left him for the white gambler, and that he had gotten drunk and gone over across the tracks in Harrison and cried and begged her to take him back, and it was then, I heard, she would get drunk and read his love letters to the white boys who came to her whorehouse. That everyone in Harrison was laughing about it, and I was too mortified to go into Harrison even to shop, and it was then I made Hunter get me my own car and a chauffeur so I could ride sixty miles into Houston to shop. Mrs. Carter used to ride with me and we would spend the day shopping together or I would, as she never had the money to buy the least thing. She wrote poems in Negro dialect and somehow she scraped up the money to get them printed. She thought it might be the beginning of her fortune, but my God, the poor thing didn't sell more than fifteen copies of her book. I bought ten of them — she had to give the rest away. Five hundred in all, as birthday and Christmas presents. She wasn't much of a poet, to tell you the truth, but she was sweet and loyal as a friend.

Anyway, I felt no shame before her, and every time I would hear something about Hunter and Maude I would ask her to find out if it was true and she would. I never asked her who she asked to find out things from ... asked her husband, no doubt. Anyway, that's when I knew that Walker, the gambler, was killed. Maude was drunk all the time grieving over him and was getting fat and losing her looks, they said. And Hunter was staying home for supper then, but he'd be in bed asleep by eight o'clock, as he was always up by four-thirty in the morning. And that was the first time I remember his calling us old. He didn't say it to me, I overheard him talking to his brother and he said, "You know, Myrtle and I are getting old," and I looked up at him and I realized he was sixty and I was fifty-six. Although he rode a horse all day and worked as hard as ever, he was almost sixty and my hair was gray now and I was in my fifties. That was the age then when people considered you old at sixty. I thought, it's 1934 and we've been married thirty-four years, and I'll go crazy if I go on sitting out here with no one to talk to but Turk, the cook, and Mrs. Carter, and listen to her dialect poetry and so I told Hunter, Depression or not, I had to get away for a while or I'd go crazy, and he'd have the expense of keeping me locked up in Austin in the asylum the rest of his life. And he said he couldn't understand that. He said if you wanted to drive him crazy, take him away from here, as he had never been farther than Harrison but four times in his life. Twice to Houston and twice to San Antonio and he didn't ever care if he never even saw Harrison again now, and never left here.

But, I guess he thought I meant it about going crazy, for the next day at breakfast there was a check for a thousand dollars by my plate and he said I could go off as long as that lasted and in those days it could last a long time. I went to visit both my daughters and I got a shock, because one of them, Lorena, told me that she and her sister thought my place was out there with Hunter and that if I hadn't gone off and left him to go traveling around Europe in the first place he wouldn't have acted the way he did and carried on so scandalously with a mulatto field hand, because that's all Maude was before he took up with her. You never knew my daughters, did you? They're both dead now. They both died before you came here to be with me. Lois found out about husbands like I said, long before she died, and I often wondered too, then, if she still agreed with Lorena that it would have made a difference if I'd stayed home, but I didn't ever say anything to her on the subject, except listen to her troubles when she told me how humiliated she was by her husband's unfaithfulness.

Anyway, when my thousand dollars was finally gone and I had

to come back here, I found Hunter still eating his supper here every night and not going out, but getting to bed by eight and Turk said that's how he acted the whole time I was gone. He said to her he was an old man now and his roaming days were over. We were in the Second World War then … And we had German prisoners out at the fairground. I drove into town with my chauffeur, who could barely read or write, so the Army wouldn't take him, to see them. There were soldiers from all over, up North, and everyplace in Harrison then and I remember back to the First World War and I had gone to a dance at the Opera House with Hunter, although he wouldn't dance. He just sat on the side all evening and watched me dancing, and he was forty-two and I was thirty-eight.

(Rear projection: portrait of Captain Lawson.) There was a captain, a Captain Lawson, who was in his early thirties, dashing and quite handsome and he gave me quite a rush all evening and he was a wonderful dancer and I know he was infatuated with me, because he wrote me a note telling me so, and I wanted badly to slip away somewhere and meet him. But I didn't dare and I got mad at Hunter and I told him what I wanted to do. That I thought it was unfair because he could openly go across the tracks and out to the cabins to his Negro woman and I couldn't be allowed to meet Captain Lawson, who was attractive and found me fascinating. And I told Hunter, hoping it would make him jealous, I suppose, and he said, "You don't fool with white women, white ladies," I believe he said …

And I said, "Look at Miss Stella Dow, she is white and she gets drunk and sleeps with who she likes."

And he says, "Do you want people to talk about you like they do Stella Dow?"

And I said no, I guess I didn't. And I don't, of course, so I never answered Captain Lawson's note and he married Vivian Fairbain, who was a young widow in town with two children. It was her son that was so brutally murdered by Junior Dawson — cut from here to here and thrown on the steps of the Caney Valley Hospital and left to bleed to death. But that's another long and tragic story and anyway, Captain Lawson and Vivian were married and lived together three years, although without his uniform he didn't seem glamorous or handsome at all. He never could get much of a job and she divorced him and took her first married name back, which was sensible since it was the name of her two children. She behaved as scandalously with men then as Miss Stella Dow, they say, and it must be something in her family, because they say Sooky, her oldest sister, went to Houston and became a prostitute.

Anyway, where was I? In the Second World War riding out to see the German prisoners and thinking about Captain Lawson. And thinking these soldiers looked young enough to be my grandsons, most of them, and I had my niece, Baby Sister, with me and Elsie, her mother, says that's when I saw that girl, Iris, because when we came back from the ride Baby Sister told her mother that we had passed this Iris and she had waved to us, but, of course, I didn't know who she was at the time and paid no attention to her at all.

(She looks at herself in the mirror.) Mr. Frohman wanted to put me on the stage in 1910 when I met him in New York City at a fabulous party. With my beauty, he said, "You must go on the stage."

"Must I?" I said.

"You must!" he said. But I didn't. I had my two little girls then. I couldn't leave them even for Mr. Frohman.

Lily Cahill went on the stage, you know, and became a famous actress. Her sister, who lived in San Antonio, was my best friend for many years. Her cousin was Katherine Anne Porter, the writer. Oh, but I've told you that. Oh, yes, where was I? Oh, yes. I was telling you about seeing the girl and not being aware I saw her. Or having not known who she was if I had been aware of it. I never saw her, you know, when I would have known who she was. Anyway I didn't know who she was or what she was doing with Hunter until after the killing. The first I knew was that someone, I forget who, came running in here and said that Hunter had killed a man in Harrison. *(She goes to the window and looks out.)*

It was in the house across the road there that Little Brother killed his father. They've torn the house down now, because no one could bear to live in it afterwards. I was sitting here when it happened. I heard the pistol shots and I thought someone was hunting close to the house and then I heard Elsie and then a Negro woman scream and then my cook, Turk, scream and she came running in here and she said Little Brother had killed his daddy.

"And he has a gun still and God knows who else he's gonna kill now. Lock the doors," she said.

But I couldn't lock the door hearing Elsie scream across the street that way and I found the strength to go to her. Stevens' face was blown away and he lay on the floor of their living room. She hovered over him screaming and I went to the phone and called our doctor in Harrison and told him to find Hunter and the sheriff and by that time Little Leon and his wife came over, but Sally wouldn't come because she had stopped speaking by then to all her brothers. She wouldn't go to the funeral either and after Little Brother had been arrested and sent to the asylum, they said it was Sally sent him the money to bribe the guards to let him get away. That was a time let me tell you. He was loose from the asylum and all of us were afraid he'd come back to kill us. Especially Elsie, his mother, because as she says it was she he was trying to kill in the first place and not Stevens. She said he came out in his underwear with the gun and said he was going to kill her, when Stevens shoved her into the next room and the boy shot him instead. He was loose for five years before they caught him again. He got into a fight in a bar up North some place and shot a man and that's how they found him and they sent him to the penitentiary up there. *(A pause.)* In the North. *(A pause.)*

Well, I outlived Hunter. That's one thing I did. He rode horseback every day pretty near up to the day he died but I outlived him. *(A pause.)*

Mr. Frohman met me at a party when I was only thirty. He told me I had great beauty and I should be on the stage. Mr. Frohman made Maude Adams a great star, of course. When he died she left the stage; she ended up teaching drama in college. Stephens College, in Missouri. *(A pause.)* A girls' school. *(A pause.)* They say she always longed to be a nun. *(A pause.)*

The day Hunter killed the girl's father I had been in my studio out back, painting. I heard Hunter's car drive into the yard, and then I heard a lot more cars driving up, and I thought something is wrong out there, something I don't want to hear about or know about. But I knew sooner or later I would have to go out of my studio and see what all the commotion was about. But I put off going as long as I could and I began to clean all my paint brushes and to tidy up my studio, when Elsie came in and I closed the door behind her and she said she had something sad to tell me. That I must be brave, because we all had a lot of friends here and they would all stand by us. We could count on the rest of the family, too, except Sally. She knew and I knew that Sally wouldn't help any one of her brothers and sisters out. And I said, "Elsie, what is this trouble that's happened?"

"Well," she said, "it's very serious and I am afraid Hunter's killed a white man. He said he did it," she said, "in self-defense, as the man was going to kill him."

"What man?" I asked.

"You know, the father of that high school girl." "What high school girl?" I asked. "I don't know what you are talking about."

"The one," she said, "you passed going out to the fairgrounds with Baby Sister to look at the German prisoners of war."

"I don't remember passing any girl," I said.

"Oh, yes," she said. "You looked right at her, Baby Sister saw you do it."

"I don't know what you're talking about" I said.

"You don't?" she replied.

"No," I said.

"Oh, Heavens!" she said. "I'm sorry I'm going to have to be the one to tell you. I'm sorry for that." And then she proceeded to tell me. To tell me all about it.

(A pause. She points to a painting in the room. Rear projection: painting of a tree.) That's one of my paintings. These are trees. I usually paint trees. Someone said to me, "I've never seen trees that color, or that shape."

"Haven't you?" I asked. "Well, I paint how they look to me."

(A pause.) I love trees. They talk to me and tell me all their secrets. Have you noticed that pine tree in the front yard? I planted that. "You're wasting your time," people said to me. "Pine trees won't grow around here. Cotton will grow and sugarcane and pin oaks and live oaks but not pines. The soil is too rich." Well, they were wrong. *(A pause.)*

The things Elsie told me. Hunter had been with a middle-aged white woman for four years, who had gotten sixty thousand dollars out of him and then she had run off with a twenty-year-old soda jerk, who worked at Outlar's Drug Store. And he had gotten very depressed and talked all the time about being an old man after the woman he gave sixty thousand dollars to ran off with the soda jerk. Elsie said they were really very worried about him. She and Stevens almost sent for me to come back home, when one day Baby Sister came home and said that a seventeen-year-old girl in the junior class, whose father painted houses for a living and was poor as a churchmouse, drove up to school one day in a spanking brand-new red convertible. And Baby Sister said when they asked her where she got it from she said it was a present from an admirer. *(A silent, almost sullen, old Negro woman brings tea in on a tray and places it in front of Myrtle. Myrtle pours the tea.)*

Thank you, Delia. *(Delia looks at her, sighs, and goes out without looking at Jessie. Rear projection: Negro church.)*

When that lady dancer from New York came out here to visit the Negro church she said the pastor welcomed her as being from the North and after the sermon he had the choir sing Negro spirituals for her. She said she had never seen such poverty in her life. She said the poverty she saw around her in that church made her cry. *(Rear projection: a series of Negro portraits — men and women.)* She said she hoped they thought it was their music that was making her cry and not the looks of them. They're still poor you know. They live, oh, I don't know how most of them live. Their houses leak, cold in winter; hot in summer. Maybe education will help. Think it will? I thought Hunter would die the day they let them go to school with the white children. You, of all people, I thought to myself, objecting to something like that. But I didn't say anything.

(Rear projection: a series of portraits of Hunter as a young man and as an older man.) I learned a long time ago not to bring up unpleasant subjects. It got you nowhere, and you could never win with him. He would just not answer whatever you said, or get up and leave the house and ride off some place on that horse of his. Oh, not that I always held my tongue. Sometimes the very sight of him would set me wild with hate and bitterness and I would begin just screaming at him of all the terrible things he'd done to me all these years, all the hurts and the humiliations and the neglect. But you know, the other night I couldn't sleep and I woke up and there was a terrible wind storm, and I thought for a moment the house would be blown away with it. But I was too tired to get up and I lay there listening to that terrible wind and thinking about Hunter and my life with him as I always seem to do in the night when I can't sleep and I thought of him dead and in his coffin and my living on, and no one now to blame my bitterness and my resentment on except a dead man. And lying in that bed, listening to the sound of that wind, the bitterness began to rise up inside me and I began to scream out again all my old grievances I held against him. I was screaming so loud that Miss Morisey, who was staying with me then, heard me over the sound of the wind and came in to me. She thought, she said, I was being murdered.

"I am," I said. "Poisoned by the memories of him. It's been a long, slow poisoning I must admit," I said, "but it is poisoning me all the same."

She sat by my bedside and I told her all about it, just as I'm now trying to tell you. And I thought to myself, if I can only even get it finally told, then I can die, too, get some rest perhaps from this burden of hate and bitterness. For I do hate him, you know, even though he's dead. I still hate him, or love him perhaps. One of his sisters said to me once, "No, you don't hate him, you love him, or you wouldn't feel such bitterness toward him." I used to tell him all the time, "God damn you, Hunter, I hate you!" But I don't believe he even cared then, what I thought or said.

(In the distance, Negro church music is heard again.) After Little Brother killed Stevens, his father, he ran across the prairie in his underwear still holding the gun.

"It was him or me," he said as he ran across the prairie.

That is what he'd heard Hunter say after he shot that seventeen-year-old white girl's father. "Him or me ... I did it in self-defense ... It was him or me."

And Little Brother was screaming that, too, as he ran into the Negro church holding his gun over his head. "I did it in self-defense, it was him or me."

And when the Negroes saw him run into that church in his underwear screaming, "It was him or me ... I did it in self-defense," they almost killed themselves getting out of that church and ran in every direction in the night across the prairie. I've thought of that night a lot sitting here. And sometimes I can see that boy, he was only twenty, just as vividly, running across the prairie holding the gun and screaming, as if I had actually seen him. Why did he do it? I ask myself ... Why did a twenty-year-old boy kill his father ... who would have killed his mother if he could have first gotten to her?

Once when I got mad at Hunter I said, "You are responsible ... You gave him the idea when you killed the father of that seventeen-year-old whore you were keeping, and he heard you saying, 'It was self-defense. It was him or me.' And he saw that you got off scot-free, no one punished you for anything, you never saw the inside of a jail or a courtroom for killing that girl's father."

That was the only time I thought he might strike me when I yelled those things at him. He started to, but he didn't. He put on his hat and walked out into the yard and he stood looking across

17

the road at the house where Stevens had lived, where he was killed, murdered, by his oldest son. And I went to the window and looked at him standing there in the yard, looking across at the house, and I felt sorry for him then, as I did when he came home after he killed the girl's father, surrounded by his friends and their wives, all of them saying they believed him that it was self-defense. He looked old and whipped-down for the first time that I can remember and in spite of their saying they believed why he did it, he just kept repeating over and over: "It was him or me." And after a while he asked all his friends and their wives to leave. He asked me to stay alone in the room with him; they all left and I stayed alone with him and he said then he was sorry for all the misery and the unhappiness he had caused me and that he was going to make it up to me. He wanted to spend the rest of his life here on earth in peace. I said, I shouldn't have I guess, but I did: "What if they kill you? What if they kill you for killing that seventeen-year-old whore's father? You won't have many days to spend in peace then," I said.

And do you know what he said? He said, "She wasn't a whore. Please don't talk that way about her. She loved me and I loved her."

"You mean to tell me you're fool enough to believe a seventeen-year-old girl loves a sixty-eight-year-old man?"

"She loved me," he said.

"Does she love you now?" I said, "Now that you've killed her daddy?"

"I don't know," he said. "I don't know about now."

And then he began to say over and over like he did to his friends. "It was self-defense. It was him or me." And finally he stopped saying it, and looked up at me and he said, "You believe that don't you?"

And I said: "Do you want the truth?"

He said, "Yes."

And I said, "No, I don't."

"It's true," he said, "He told me to stop seeing her or he'd kill me."

"He didn't even have a gun on him," I said.

"But I didn't know that," he said. "I saw him coming toward me and I thought for sure he had a gun and I killed him. They believe me," he said.

"Who does?" I said.

"My friends," he said.

"Do they?" I asked.

"Yes," he said. "You heard them say they did."

"And what about his friends?" I said. "What do they believe?"

"What friends?" he said. "He's shiftless and no 'count and just a house painter. What friends does he have?"

And I guess he didn't have many, if any. Anyway, they say only six or seven people came to his funeral when they buried him in Harrison and the day after the funeral they had some kind of hearing over at the courthouse which Hunter didn't even have to attend. His brother, Stevens, and Little Brother went as his representatives. And he had a lawyer there, of course, and Stevens told the judge how Hunter said it happened. That the seventeen-year-old girl's father had threatened his life. What was that man's name? I can't remember ... I think it was Gallagher or Gallaway or ... Anyway, I remember her name, it was Iris.

Anyway, he was acquitted at that hearing of any wrong doing. And someone said Hunter gave a hundred thousand dollars to Iris and her mother and they left town. But someone else told me it was ten and someone else five. I asked him once how much he paid them to leave. He said he had paid them nothing; there was nothing to pay them for. Anyway, they left, rode away in that red convertible he had given her, I reckon, rode away and vanished.

(Rear projection: a young white girl.) I'd never seen her, of course, that I remembered, in spite of what Elsie thought, until one day five or six years later when I was shopping in Foley's in Houston with Elsie. She said, "There she is."

"There's who?" I asked.

"Iris," she said. "The girl whose father Hunter killed."

She was working in the bridal department there in the store. It was her job, one of the clerks told me, to go around and show customers how to put on weddings, big, formal weddings, the clerk said. Sometimes she models different wedding gowns for the customers, the clerk said. Because of her beauty, she said, "She can make any gown, no matter how tacky, desirable. Don't you think she's beautiful?" the clerk asked me.

"Do you want an honest opinion?" I said.

"Why, yes," the clerk said.

"Yes, I guess I do. In a common sort of way," I said. "However, common beauty has never appealed to me."

"She's had a very sad life," the clerk said. "Her father was murdered in cold blood by a rich man over in Harrison, who was in love with her and wanted to marry her. But he had a devil of a wife and she wouldn't give him a divorce and so her father said if that rich man couldn't marry her, she had to stop seeing him. The rich man got in a rage when he said that and killed him. Got off scot-free, too.

"Then she came to Houston and married a man whose family had a lot of money. One of the Lee boys, Jack or Lester, I can't remember which." And then she turned to the sales girl next to her and asked, as if I cared, who Iris married … Jack or Lester Lee?

And the girl said, "Lester," and then she said his family wouldn't give him any money, rich as they were, because he drank so. So she had to go to work to support them, since he was born and raised a rich boy and didn't, consequently, know how to do anything and here she was.

"Is she still married to Lester Lee?" Elsie asked her, as if it mattered.

And the woman said no. She had to leave him finally on account of his drinking. She was being courted now by an oil millionaire and she heard the other day that somebody wanted to send her out to Hollywood and make her a movie star. Well, she never got to Hollywood, of course, at least if she did she never made any pictures, not any I ever heard of, that is. God knows where she is now, or what's become of her. Her mother became a call girl they say. David Meyers told Elsie that and Elsie told me. She said he used to go to the Lamar Hotel to get women and they would always send four or five women up to your room for you to choose from and one night he said one of the women that came up was Martha Davis that used to slip off from her husband and children and go into Houston and work as a call girl. Although I'm not sure she really slipped off. Some people said her husband knew all about it and didn't care. Anyway, he said he'd hardly gotten over the shock of seeing Martha when he saw standing next to her Iris's mother.

"How's Iris?" he asked her.

"Gone to the dogs," she said.

But that was just the mother talking, because Elsie told me, just before she died when she went to New Orleans for the Sugar Bowl Game, she saw Iris big as life and she was well-dressed and with a good-looking man who seemed to have lots of money. Elsie said she was still pretty enough to be in pictures. A little matronly-looking now but very pretty.

I was a beauty, too, many people think when I was younger. Mr. Daniel Frohman, I think he went down with the *Titanic*, didn't he?

I believe so. And it broke Maude Adams' heart they tell me and she retired from the stage after he died. He treated her like a princess, you know. He made a great star of her. I saw her do *Peter Pan* and *A Kiss for Cinderella*, and later, after he died and she retired, she decided to try the stage again and she teamed with Otis Skinner in *The Merchant of Venice*. I went to see her in that when she came to Houston.

Mr. Frohman begged me to go on the stage when he met me. "I have a husband and two little girls," I said.

"No matter," he said. "Your beauty should not be wasted, it belongs to the world."

Anyway, once I got to thinking about the man Hunter killed, I went out to the graveyard in Harrison to look for his grave, but then I remembered I'd never overheard his name. So, I asked Red, my chauffeur, what was the name of the man that Hunter killed.

"It was Davis," he said, "Lovell Davis."

"Go out there and see if you can find his grave," I said.

He looked around the graveyard for a better part of an hour and when he came back he said he had finally found it. I got out of the car and followed him to where the grave was and a tombstone had just been put up recently and marked on it was, "Rest in Peace Daddy, Love Iris." *(A pause.)* And the date of his birth and the day he died. *(A pause.)* He was thirty-five when he was shot and killed by Hunter. She was seventeen, which meant he was eighteen when she was born.

"Where did they come from?" I asked Red.

"I don't know, ma'am," he said, "nor where they gone to."

"Well, we know where he's gone to," I said. "In a coffin in Harrison, buried deep in the ground."

"Yes, ma'am," he said.

And of course, that's where Hunter had ended — in a coffin, not in Harrison, but in Egypt. Like Joseph in the Bible. The difference between Joseph and Hunter was he would have lain with Potiphar's wife. Do you know how the first chapter of Genesis begins? "In the beginning God created Heaven and Earth." And how the book ends? "In a coffin in Egypt." That's where I'll end too, of course, next to Hunter and my two daughters in a coffin in Egypt. Someone said the mulatto, Maude Jenkins, sent word from California to her people here that when she dies she wants to be shipped back here and buried in Egypt, too. Of course, she won't be buried in our

21

graveyard, but with the colored people, with her family ... which there were a lot of, and they say she's been wonderful to all her kin, her sisters and brothers and their children. Sent them food and clothes and educated them that wanted it. But no matter, she will end up, too, like the rest of us, won't she? Black and white. In a coffin in Egypt or some place. *(A pause.)*

If I could have one day to live over before I die, do you know what I'd choose? *(A pause.)* I'd choose one of those lovely clear spring days we used to have out here when I came here first as a bride and I'd get on my horse and ride across the prairie at sunrise to the east and ride all day on and on ... *(She gets up, goes to the bookcase.)*

Here are two books of Katherine Anne Porter. ... *Flowering Judas* and *Pale Horse, Pale Rider. (She takes them out of the bookcase and shows them to Jessie.)*

This is her picture. She was quite beautiful, wasn't she? Lily Cahill was her cousin. Lily played with Jane Cowl in *First Lady*, and she always knew how to dress very smartly, both onstage and off. And she toured, you know, all over America in *Life with Father.* Then she couldn't get work and she had to go back to San Antonio, Texas. I don't believe she was ever in a Frohman production. I could have been, you know. Mr. Frohman said he could have made a great star of me. He said I had the temperament to be a very great actress. And the beauty, and the poise. And the clothes ... I always had, if I do say so myself, a remarkable sense of what looked best on me. Red was my favorite color. But I didn't wear it often, until my hair was white, and then I did and with great effect. Red hats, large-brimmed; red coats; red dresses; red shoes. I adored red. I surrounded myself in red. Red clothes, red furnishings ...

"Red is a whore's color," someone said to me once.

"But if I wear it, it's a lady's color," I said.

"Oh, yes," she said, "for you are a lady, there is no mistaking that. Always a lady."

"Except with Hunter," I said. "He gets me so angry I forget myself, forget I am a lady, forget ... " *(The Negro music is heard again.)*

Turk was not in church that night Little Brother ran in there in his underwear, waving the gun, but her husband was and her sister was. She hadn't gone because she knew I was very despondent after Hunter had killed that man, Iris's father, and she said she was not going to leave me feeling like that.

"Oh, I've been despondent a great deal of my life, Turk," I said, "I'm used to it."

"Not like now," she said. "I've never seen you like now," she said. And I think she was right. I felt a depth of humiliation those days that I'd never known before or since. And so I locked myself in my room and Turk brought me my meals. Not that I could eat anything at all, and I was in my room alone, not crying, but feeling a grief like I've never known before or since. When I heard Elsie scream and Turk ran in to tell me what the screams were about. *(A pause. She glances toward the window.)*

"A coffin in Egypt" … That's where Hunter is, and Stevens and my two girls all buried right out there with their father and grandfather and great-grandfather and even Sally, who wouldn't speak to any of them for twenty years before she died, is buried out there beside them. But Little Brother, where is he? Up North some place in a prison … Minnesota, Wisconsin, Idaho … some place where it's cold and it snows all winter long. That's where they have him locked up. After they caught him finally living some way up there, who, as far as I know had never done a day's work in his life. Living up there, working up there, if he did work, which I doubt, since I think Sally was sending him money all the time. Just like I think it was Sally who paid off the guards to let him escape from the asylum in Austin.

"Why in the name of God would she do something like that?" Turk said when I told her my opinion of the situation.

"Because she's got a mean streak in her," I said. "Had since girlhood, hates her brothers and their wives, bitter, I've always thought that, because she couldn't have children of her own." The only one of the family she ever cared about was Little Brother. Doted on him. Absolutely … Always telling him how his mother and daddy favored Baby Sister over him and how he never got his fair share from his mother and father or any of the rest of us. Elsie says she thinks she poisoned his mind and that's why he went off that way and did what he did. Anyway, we were all scared to death, let me tell you, after he ran away from the asylum and we didn't know for five years where he was. It was a time of terror around here. No matter what happened or what you did always in the back of your mind was that this night might just be the night that he would take it in his head to come back here and kill the rest of us. I was scared as the rest of them. We were all scared except Sally, and she wasn't scared, I've always felt, because she knew where he was and what he was up to, since she was sending him the money.

"Can you prove that?" Hunter said once when I told him what I felt.

"No," I said, "but there are a lot of things I know that I can't prove. Like, I know you haven't learned your lesson by getting caught running around with a seventeen-year-old girl. You already have yourself another woman over in Harrison some place."

"How do you figure that?" he said.

"Because I know you, Hunter," I said …

(A pause.) I don't know where they buried Captain Lawson, or even where he died. Did he die in Harrison? I can't remember. Anyway, I don't think so. I think he moved away after Vivian divorced him. I have never seen a man change so in my life when he took that uniform off. Everybody still called him "Captain," but it sounded funny because he was clerking in a grocery store for Mr. Sam Borden. Women would go in and say, "Captain Lawson, how are the mustard greens today?" Or, "the Irish Potatoes?" Or whatever. And he'd click his heels and bow just like he was still in the army, only he looked funny clicking his heels and bowing with his butcher's apron on. Captain Lawson. What was his first name? Ernest? Albert? I can't remember. Captain Lawson. Long, long ago. He is dead and Vivian is dead. She's buried in the Harrison cemetery, but I'm not sure where he is buried.

(A pause.) I was in this room when I heard a noise outside and said, "Turk, get in here and lock all the doors and windows, he's back."

"Oh, my God!" she said, because she knew who I meant. I meant Little Brother. "Are you sure?" she said.

"Yes, I heard his footsteps around the side of the house."

But it wasn't Little Brother, because we read next morning in the Houston paper how he had gotten into a fight up North in a bar and tried to kill a man and the police came and arrested him and found out he was escaped from the asylum in Austin, Texas. Later the man died. I hear they gave Little Brother life. I am sorry about the man dying, but I'm glad they caught Little Brother and locked him up for life. And not even Sally could get him out of there, no matter what she was willing to spend. His name was never mentioned after that, by his mother or his sister or his uncles. Now they're all dead. I don't know if they ever wrote to him, or heard from him ever again. I thought the other night … What does he think about being locked up in that prison in the North? I haven't seen him since he was twenty, and if he walked in this yard tomorrow, he would be an old man and I wouldn't know him. And I thought if he died who would they get in touch with? Me? Or would they? Maybe he is dead and buried in a coffin in wherever he is. What do they do with them when they die in those prisons? Do they send them home to their people like when they're killed in the army? Or do they bury them there in the prison? I'd write up there and find out if he was dead or alive, if I knew who to write to. Bud Jackson was sheriff then and might know where he was. Bud told me once in all the years he was sheriff catching that boy was one of the hardest things he ever had to do. He said it was even harder than going to California and getting Dude Borden when he was paroled out of San Quentin and bringing him back here, because he was raised with Dude and Dude was his best friend when he was a boy, although Dude was supposed to be off of dope in San Quentin, he knew he wasn't, and he knew that taking him to Houston was just like turning him over to the dope peddlers, which it was. Because Bud said in three weeks he was back on it full-force. He never sold it again, though, which was what they arrested him for doing in California.

Anyway, I was out in the yard when they told Bud about Stevens being killed and Little Brother running across the prairie somewhere, and he told Hunter that he would catch him, and he hoped he would come peacefully, because he didn't intend to get killed and he would kill him if Little Brother started shooting at him. Some Negroes came up then and told him he had come into the church hollering, "It was him or me." And as far as they knew he was still in the church so Bud and his deputies started for the church.

They surrounded it first and then called for him to come out, but he didn't come out because he wasn't in it by the time they got there. They rode all night across the prairie, their lights flashing in every direction, until finally they found him sprawled across the ground so sound asleep he didn't hear the cars until they were up beside him. He didn't holler or struggle, he just looked up at Bud from where he lay on the ground and he said, Bud told us later, just as calm, "I want you to hear my side of it, Bud. I did it in self-defense. It was him or me."

"That may be," Bud said he told him, "but get up now, Little Brother, like a good boy and come with me."

"Where are you taking me?" Little Brother said.

"Where I have to take you," Bud said. "To the jail in Harrison."

"Why?" Little Brother asked him.

"Because you killed your daddy," Bud told him.

"I know that," Little Brother said. "But why are you locking me up? You didn't lock up Uncle Hunter when he killed that man."

Hunter was standing beside me when he told me that, and I thought to myself, I hope you are listening Hunter, and I looked up at Hunter's face. His expression hadn't changed one iota. He just listened and nodded his head like he was one of the wise men from the East.

They didn't have a trial for Little Brother either, but declared him insane. A colored man Turk knew said he had the cell next to Little Brother and he said on the day of his daddy's funeral Little Brother had gotten a funeral notice some way and he was reading it out loud from his cell. He said to that colored man that they were burying his daddy today and he had killed him in self-defense, but that nobody had come to see him in jail but his Aunt Sally. And she did come, too, because the colored man saw her and heard her say she was going to stand by him. *(A pause.)*

The fall isn't much here. Oh, it's nice if you have pecan trees and there is a good crop, but it's hot as summer a lot of the fall, except when a norther blows up across the prairie and then it can get cold let me tell you. It's the northers blow all the pecans out of these trees. And you can see people scurrying around raking through the leaves looking for the pecans. I never did, of course, the Negroes always picked mine up for me. Oh, and the winters. Deliver me! Rains, it seems to me, all winter long. But, oh, the spring is lovely. The wildflowers are beautiful then, primroses and buttercups and Indian blankets, but I told you about those. And did I tell you about Mr. Frohman wanting to put me on the stage? I told Hunter that. "He's some kind of a damn fool," Hunter said. *(A pause.)*

"The Angel that talked with me came again, and waked me, as a man that's wakened out of his sleep." I woke up last night thinking of that, that's from the Bible some place. *(A pause.)* Lily Cahill got to be a star, too. Not under Mr. Frohman, though. Maude Adams was his star. Is she dead or alive? Someone told me the other day Katherine Anne Porter was still alive. If she is, she's as old as I am. As old as I am. I could write a book let me tell you. What a book I could write. *(A pause.)* "The Angel that talked with me came again … " That's in Zechariah some place, I think. *(A pause.)*

The mulatto, Maude Jenkins, came back here one time in the forties they say. In a brand-new Cadillac, more expensive than anything Hunter or I ever owned, and she drove it slowly around the courthouse square so everybody could see she was prospering out there in California. *(A pause.)*

They tore the house down piece by piece where Little Brother killed his father. The plants that surrounded the house, the oleander and the crepe myrtle and rose bushes, they left standing, and the trees in the yard. *(A pause.)* I left home the day they began to take the house down. Where did I go that time? *(A pause.)* Hunter called me when it was all done. "The house is down," he said, "you can come home now," and I did. *(A pause.)*

Hand me that book yonder by Katherine Anne Porter, *Flowering Judas*. I think I'll read one of her stories. *(Jessie hands her the book. Myrtle opens it.)* She had several husbands you know. Two or three, I don't remember. Lily Cahill never married. Mr. Frohman married, but Maude Adams never did. They say ... Well, you know how they talk. Anyway, I don't believe a word of it. Mr. Frohman always behaved in a very gentlemanly fashion with me, and I think he had a very deep interest in spiritual things. *(A pause.)*

The day Hunter died was a cold, bleak November day. He just went to sleep sitting in his chair there. We buried him the next day. It rained, so not many people came out from Harrison. Just his brother and his wife and his nephews and their wives, and me, of course, and a few neighbors and the rest were blacks. Every black out this way and there are enough of them. Why was that? He was mean as the devil to most of them. And not just the old ones: the young, too. *(The Negro singing is heard.)*

Who is left to come to my funeral? *(A pause.)* I'm older by twenty years than the mulatto, Maude Jenkins, but I've outlived so many, I might outlive her. Who will come to her funeral? There will be lots of Jenkins there, because they are still thick in the county and the blacks will come from everywhere from all the bottoms and the prairies, out of curiosity if nothing else. *(A pause.)* And I'd like to go just to get a look at her after all these years. But I couldn't, of course, even if I was still alive then. *(A pause.)*

"The Angel that talked with me came again, and waked me, as a man that's wakened out of his sleep." *(A pause.)* "The Angel that talked with me came again, and waked me, as a man that's wakened out of his sleep." *(A pause.)*

What was the name of Mr. Frohman's theater? The Empire. It was across the street from the Metropolitan Opera House. They're both torn down I read somewhere. I attended them both. Many times. I loved New York. I loved Paris. I loved Algiers. I loved Rome. I loved … Egypt. Not, Egypt, Texas, but Egypt. Egypt … Magic, Egypt. I used to tell Hunter that when I died I wanted to be cremated and have my ashes taken to one of the beautiful places I'd known as a young woman. But now, I don't care. Who is there left to take my ashes anywhere? Anyway, they have a place for my body between Hunter's grave and my two girls and that's where I'll end. In a coffin in Egypt. This Egypt. Out on the prairie. And in the spring our graves will be covered with the wildflowers, with primroses and Indian blankets and bluebonnets. *(A pause.)*

What was the name of the man that Hunter killed? Gallagher? Or Gallaway? No … No … That's not it. I thought of it earlier. It wasn't an Irish name. It was English … Davis … Yes. Lovell Davis. That's right. Now who in the name of God was Gallagher or Gallaway? *(A pause.)* No matter. *(A pause.)*

Mr. Frohman said, "I can't believe you are the mother of these two children … Why you seem more like their sister." Where is he buried? And Maude Adams? And Lily Cahill? And Katherine Anne Porter? And … Listen … Hear the wind out on the prairie? I think it will storm tonight. I never mind them you know. Storms comfort me somehow. *(A pause.)* Gallaway was the name of the first white child born in Harrison, someone told me once. *(A pause.)*

"Tell us another one," Hunter said. *(A pause.)*

"Another what?" I said. *(A pause.)*

"Another one of your lies," he said, "about Mr. Frohman and a Sheikh being in love with you."

"He was," I said.

"And Captain Lawson … and … " *(A pause.)*

Hunter … He never said he loved me. He said I can never say things like that, but he wrote them to Maude Jenkins, in those letters from him she would get drunk and read to the white boys. Oh, so long ago.

"I hate you, Hunter." That's what I told him. Over and over. … "I hate you." Did I? Was he ever here in this room? In that chair? Riding his horse across those fields? Was I young once? A girl? Was I in France and Algiers and New York? Was I? Was there a Captain Lawson and did he flirt with me? And Mr. Frohman? Did he want me to become an actress? And what if I had and left Hunter and my two girls? How would it all have ended? Anyway, I've outlived Hunter and Mr. Frohman and Lily Cahill and Maude Adams and Katherine Anne Porter … *(She closes her eyes. She opens them.)*

Lovell Davis. Not Gallagher or Gallaway. Lovell Davis was the name of the man Hunter killed. Iris Davis was his daughter. She was the seventeen-year-old girl Hunter had an affair with when he was sixty-eight … *(A pause.)* I never saw Lovell Davis that I remembered. Not even a picture, but, of course, I might have passed him on the streets of Harrison without knowing who he was. I saw Iris once in Houston working in Foley's. But I told you that. *(A pause.)*

"The Angel that talked with me came again … " And I visited the grave of Lovell Davis once, but I told you that. *(A pause.)*

Renee Gordon's husband, Jason, got mixed up with a seventeen-year-old girl once in Harrison and the father of the girl threatened to kill him and he wasn't of Hunter's stripe at all, so he left town. Renee felt so disgraced over the whole thing that she killed herself. Hung herself. Not me. I felt disgraced all right, but I never once thought of killing myself. *(A pause.)* I wouldn't give Hunter that satisfaction. *(A pause.)*

"Myrtle," she said, "this is Mr. Frohman. He asked to be introduced to you."

"You are the loveliest one here tonight," he said.

"Thank you," I said.

"Have you ever considered a career in the theater?" Mr. Frohman said.

"As an actress?" I asked.

"Yes," he said.

"Heavens no," I said.

I was beautiful then, you know. I was a very great beauty then. I had exquisite hands and lovely tiny feet … and … I had style. "I can't teach you a thing about clothes," Lily Cahill said to me. "You have more style than anyone I know." *(The Negroes sing in the distance.)*

Running across the prairie in his underwear … "It was him or me. Self-defense." The Negroes scattered like partridges. They all disappeared into the night and left him alone in the church of God … Screaming, "It was him or me." *(A pause.)*

Oh, the days and the years, summer and winter … spring and fall … *(A pause.)* The spring is my favorite time. In the spring … when I was a girl. A long, long time ago, when I was a girl, a bride,

29

and I came here, before … Anyway, I've told you all that. *(She begins to read again from the book. She closes her eyes.)* Yes, I've told you all that. What else? Hunter and me. I was nineteen when he proposed in a buggy taking me to my home in Eagle Lake, Texas. In a buggy, a surrey … and he was rich, they said, and I was beautiful and intelligent and … *(A pause. She opens her eyes. She turns and looks out the window. Curtain.)*

End of Play

PROPERTY LIST

Book
Tea service for two
Fashion magazine

NEW PLAYS

★ **AGES OF THE MOON by Sam Shepard.** Byron and Ames are old friends, reunited by mutual desperation. Over bourbon on ice, they sit, reflect and bicker until fifty years of love, friendship and rivalry are put to the test at the barrel of a gun. "A poignant and honest continuation of themes that have always been present in the work of one of this country's most important dramatists, here reconsidered in the light and shadow of time passed." –NY Times. "Finely wrought…as enjoyable and enlightening as a night spent stargazing." –Talkin' Broadway. [2M] ISBN: 978-0-8222-2462-4

★ **ALL THE WAY by Robert Schenkkan. Winner of the 2014 Tony Award for Best Play.** November, 1963. An assassin's bullet catapults Lyndon Baines Johnson into the presidency. A Shakespearean figure of towering ambition and appetite, this charismatic, conflicted Texan hurls himself into the passage of the Civil Rights Act—a tinderbox issue emblematic of a divided America—even as he campaigns for re-election in his own right, and the recognition he so desperately wants. In Pulitzer Prize and Tony Award–winning Robert Schenkkan's vivid dramatization of LBJ's first year in office, means versus ends plays out on the precipice of modern America. ALL THE WAY is a searing, enthralling exploration of the morality of power. It's not personal, it's just politics. "…action-packed, thoroughly gripping… jaw-dropping political drama." –Variety. "A theatrical coup…nonstop action. The suspense of a first-class thriller." –NY1. [17M, 3W] ISBN: 978-0-8222-3181-3

★ **CHOIR BOY by Tarell Alvin McCraney.** The Charles R. Drew Prep School for Boys is dedicated to the creation of strong, ethical black men. Pharus wants nothing more than to take his rightful place as leader of the school's legendary gospel choir. Can he find his way inside the hallowed halls of this institution if he sings in his own key? "[An] affecting and honest portrait…of a gay youth tentatively beginning to find the courage to let the truth about himself become known." –NY Times. "In his stirring and stylishly told drama, Tarell Alvin McCraney cannily explores race and sexuality and the graces and gravity of history." –NY Daily News. [7M] ISBN: 978-0-8222-3116-5

★ **THE ELECTRIC BABY by Stefanie Zadravec.** When Helen causes a car accident that kills a young man, a group of fractured souls cross paths and connect around a mysterious dying baby who glows like the moon. Folk tales and folklore weave throughout this magical story of sad endings, strange beginnings and the unlikely people that get you from one place to the next. "The imperceptible magic that pervades human existence and the power of myth to assuage sorrow are invoked by the playwright as she entwines the lives of strangers in THE ELECTRIC BABY, a touching drama." –NY Times. "As dazzling as the dialogue is dreamful." –Pittsburgh City Paper. [3M, 3W] ISBN: 978-0-8222-3011-3

DRAMATISTS PLAY SERVICE, INC.
440 Park Avenue South, New York, NY 10016 212-683-8960 Fax 212-213-1539
postmaster@dramatists.com www.dramatists.com